Lead me in youand teach me, for you are the God of my salvation; for you I wait all the day long. Psalm 25:5

The sum of your word is truth, and every one of your righteous rules endures forever. Psalm 119:160

For the law was given
through Moses; grace and
truth came through Jesus
Christ. John 1:17

Send out your light and your truth; let them lead me; let them bring me to your holy hill and to your dwelling! Psalm 43:3

Behold, you delight in truth in the inward being, and you teach me wisdom in the secret heart. Psalm 51:6

God is spirit, and those who worship him must worship in spirit and truth. John 4:24

You will know the truth, and the truth will set you free. John 8:32

Jesus said to him, "I am the way, and the truth, and the life. No one comes to the Father except through me." John 14:6

Stand therefore, having fastened on the belt of truth, and having put on the breastplate of righteousness. Ephesians 6:14

Love does not
rejoice at
wrongdoing,
but rejoices
with the truth.
1 Corinthians 13:6

If we say we have no sin, we deceive ourselves, and the truth is not in us. 1 John 1:8

Let us not love in word or talk but in deed and in truth. By this we shall know that we are

of the truth and reassure our heart before

him; for whenever our heart condemns us, God is greater than our heart, and he knows everything.

1 John 3:18-20

Do your best to present yourself to God as one approved, a worker who has no need

to be ashamed, rightly handling the word of truth. 2 Timothy 2:15

What does the word truth mean? Truth is what is right. If something really happened then it is true. The opposite of truth is untruth or lies. Lies are sin and God tells us that we are not to have anything to do with them. God is true. Every word he says is truth. Everything about God is perfect and true. We can trust God as he will never lie to us. His word is true forever. God's truth will lead us through life in the right way.

When God tells us that he is the one true God and that there are no other gods before him, that is true. When Jesus says that he is the only way to know God the Father and that he is the only one we can trust to forgive our sins, that is true. The only way to heaven is through trusting in the Lord Jesus Christ to save us from sin. People who tell you that there are lots of ways to get to heaven are not telling the truth. There is only one real truth and that is the Word of God.